'As someone who reads about four business books each month, I can honestly say that this slim volume is packed with some of the best, practical advice I have read for a long time.' *David Cook*

'Practical, useful, but most of all cheerful. Surprising how much more readable that makes it. I hope it's very successful.' *Richard Popple, PerService Ltd*

'A most useful and enjoyable read.' *R.F. Summers, The Business Support Group*

'Some tremendous ideas for keeping in touch and building credibility.' *Andrew Lightbody, PA Consulting Group*

'Read it straight off. It's a great little book and it's more than paid for itself already by reminding me to do something important.' *Michael Rigby, Michael Rigby Associates*

'In my view it is excellent and I will recommend it to my colleagues. Your tips are appropriate for all consultants, not only those who work independently!' *Cathy Rowan, KPMG Peat Marwick*

'Anyone involved in selling will benefit. It's a real conscience-pricker. It tells you all the things you know you ought to be doing and a lot more you should have known.' *Richard Birtchnell, Managing Director, Forum Communications Ltd*

'I receive literally dozens of approaches from independent consultants. If they used just a third of the techniques that Timothy Foster recommends, their success rate would increase markedly.' *Martin Langford, Joint Managing Director, Burson-Marsteller*

'A fun read and a good book. Don't go solo without it.' *Charles Dawson, Managing Consultant, Neomedion Ltd*

'This book should greatly help those who are good to get that fact across fast.' *John de Uphaugh, Deputy Chief Executive, Dewe Rogerson Europe*

'This book is a must for every budding entrepreneur or indeed those in existing businesses.' *Harry Mannveille, National Federation of Self Employed and Small Businesses*

Other books in this series by this author:

101 WAYS TO SUCCEED AS AN INDEPENDENT CONSULTANT

This book is dedicated to
the memory of Geoff Nightingale

101 WAYS TO
SUCCEED AS AN INDEPENDENT CONSULTANT

SECOND EDITION

TIMOTHY RV FOSTER

**KOGAN
PAGE**

YOURS TO HAVE AND TO HOLD

BUT NOT TO COPY

First published in 1991
Reprinted 1992; with revisions 1995
Second edition 1999

Kogan Page Limited
120 Pentonville Road
London N1 9JN

© Timothy R V Foster 1991, 1999

British Library Cataloguing in Publication Data

A CIP record for this book is available from the British Library.

ISBN 0 7494 2962 3

Typeset by Saxon Graphics Ltd, Derby
Printed in England by Clays Ltd, St Ives plc

Contents

CONTENTS

Introduction

This book is based on my 40 years of experience working for companies and as an independent consultant in the areas of advertising, marketing, sales, public relations and training, in the UK, Canada and the United States.

This was the first book in Kogan Page's *101 Ways* series, leading to a library of 15 titles, of which I have written seven. In the seven years since it was first published we have discovered the Internet, the World Wide Web and the wonders of e-mail. And more and more people are working for themselves. So I have revised the book to recognise the realities of the new millennium. Interestingly, in the process of revision, it was pleasing to note that the strategies and techniques described then are just as valid today as they were seven years ago. *Plus ça change, plus c'est la même chose.* (The more things change, the more they stay the same.)

This book is designed to convey some of the ideas and techniques that I've found to be effective in developing and building business for myself and my clients.

What is a consultant? One type I've heard about is based on the following interchange:

Client: "What time is it?"
Consultant: "May I borrow your watch a moment? Now what time would you like it to be?"

I hope you can do better than that! (I understand in Florida now there are Leisure Consultants – people who give advice on how to spend your spare time now you've retired to the sunshine state!)

You might be a management consultant, an architect, a writer, a trainer, an engineer, a product-placement expert, a designer, a stylist, a musician, a "dress for success" specialist, a computer-systems analyst, a financial adviser or something else – if your livelihood is based on your ability to *seek, obtain* and *serve* clients, you'll find *strategies* and *techniques* to help you be more successful in this book.

One of the things you need to do is get a clear idea of your Unique Selling Proposition (USP). I've come to identify myself as a *knowledge navigator* – helping people to find their way around the wealth of information that exists in many different fields. If there is one thing I've learned to do, it's how to put a variety of ingredients together from different disciplines to produce an effective result. Some people call this *synergy,* which my dictionary defines as a combined or cooperative action or force. What's your USP?

How to Get the Most out of This Book

It's organised into eight broad sections, each containing a number of ways to progress your cause. The sections are:

- How to promote what you do
- How to keep in touch
- How to build credibility for yourself
- How to grow the relationship
- How to work with your clients in the development stage
- How to work with your clients in the ongoing stage
- How to work with your clients when you have problems
- How to put it all together

The 101 ways that are outlined here are real, based on real experiences. All the anecdotes really happened. There's no fluff to pad the book out. It's intentionally lean, to give you fast solutions to problems that you may have.

The mechanisms described here are not intended to be rigid rules. They are meant to be idea prompters. Allow yourself to apply variations as you see fit.

Start by reading the book through, from front to back. That shouldn't take you more than an hour. Have a pencil or highlighter to hand. When you come across a way that seems to be useful, circle it. Dog-ear the page. Then go back and see if you can adapt those ideas to your way of doing business. Use them as a launching pad. Some of the ideas may appear familiar to you. Fine. They are there for completeness, so you don't miss anything. But I guarantee that some of the concepts will be new to you, and I hope you find these helpful in bringing you the success you so richly deserve.

In the back of the book, you'll find a reading list and some useful addresses along with Web sites where available – just part of the added value we give you!

How to Promote What You Do

In the early days of your career, you don't have much to go on. You start with an education, some job experience and a few lucky breaks. Merge in good personal presentation and communication skills, and you are on your way. Start delivering, and you'll make a name for yourself. Then people will recommend you to their friends and you will become more successful.

The up-front problem is, it's a very competitive world out there, and there are a lot of other people trying to get at the same bones that you want to chew on. So you need to differentiate yourself. You need to identify something unique about what you do, and then find a good way to get that message in front of the right people.

Here are some ideas.

Way 1 Identify your targets

To whom should you be talking? Decision-makers in your field? People in the purchasing department? The managing director? Bear in mind that in the corporate world you may be dealing with a hierarchy of people – end-users, recommenders, specifiers, approvers and so on. You need to reach them all with appropriate signals. Identifying these categories is your first step in developing a communications programme to promote yourself. Sources of this information are people you know, network contacts, directories, and stories in the relevant media and, of course, the World Wide Web.

Way 2 Identify your Unique Selling Proposition (USP)

You need to *differentiate* yourself, so that when people think of you they automatically build in the link to your own USP. Why should someone use you rather than another person? The *reason* is your *edge*. Is it because you are there? Because you have the lowest prices? Because you know more about the subject than anyone else? Because you're fun to be with? Because you're famous?

To help you with this task, try the following exercise. Write down the names of the ten brands you most admire – cars, TVs, restaurants, services, airlines, hotels, chocolates, whiskies, whatever. Then write down the attribute you think that each brand has that makes it so. I'll give you a few of my own favourites:

- CNN (Cable News Network) – 24-hour global television news
- Federal Express – guaranteed delivery on time
- Macintosh computer – intuitive, user-friendly, graphic operation
- Virgin Atlantic Airlines – the best business class service

If you know who your competitors are, try the same thing for them. Then write down ten attributes for yourself that could be used to differentiate you from everyone else. *You* are a *brand!*

When you're clear on your USP, build it into your image. Use it in your communications, your business card, your logo, your letterhead. *Live* your USP! It should become part of your own *positioning*.

Way 3 How are you positioned in your prospects' minds?

You may be surprised to know that you are *already* positioned in their minds. Your positioning may be "Who?", but it's a positioning nevertheless. You are then lodged with the group headed "Never heard of them". Or it may be – "Oh yes, I've heard of them – what is it they do again?" You want to be in the rarefied atmosphere of total trust and reliance – "They're the greatest – absolutely top rate". You can only get there by *earning* it. *IMP*

You can only earn it by enabling your contacts to *experience* first hand what you have to offer. A succession of positive experiences will build increasing trust and a sense of your own reliability. *Negative* experiences will be very destructive. People tend to share negative experiences four times as often as they share positive experiences.

Who controls *your* positioning? You? And if not you, who? And what are you doing about it?

The key point is that you're positioned differently with different members of your audience. With your best client, your positioning is quite different from that with someone whose bag of groceries you just scattered when you bumped into them on the street.

Recognising where you stand with your different targets will help you to move yourself up the positioning ladder with each of them to a position of total trust and reliance.

And don't forget that your USP must be part of your positioning – that's why so many companies put a slogan with their logo – I call it a *slogo*. Here are three of my favourites:

- Taste. Not waist. (Weight Watchers Frozen Meals)

- Getting there is half the fun. (Cunard Steamship Lines)

- When it absolutely, positively has to be there overnight. (Federal Express)

The purpose of the slogo is to leave the key brand message in the mind of the target. It is the signature that accompanies the logo. It says 'If you get nothing else from us, get this...!'

A perfectly formed slogo should have as many of these characteristics as possible:

- it should be memorable;
- it should recall the brand name;
- it should include a key benefit;
- it should differentiate the brand;
- it should impart positive feelings about the brand;
- it should not be usable by a competitor.

Three more good slogos:

- British Telecom: 'It's good to talk'.
- 'The flavour of a Quaver is never known to waver'.
- Jaguar: 'Grace... Space... Pace...'

And three not-so-good:

- Equity & Law: 'Need we say more?'
- MFI Furniture: 'Take a look at us now'.
- Showerlux: 'No wonder we're ahead'.

Way 4 Rise above the noise

We are all inundated with communications. How can you make your message work – taking you above the general background noise? Since I write television scripts, and communicate with people in TV production companies, I devised a mailing piece that resembled a *storyboard* – the depiction of a TV script that tells the story in a series of frames. I even called it a storyboard. It produced a quarter of my total revenue in the first year I used it. Not only was the communication original, it was memorable. I could say on the phone, "I'm the chap who sent you a CV that looks like a storyboard" – instant recall! One producer who ended up giving me a lot of work said, on my first phone call to him, "I've got it right here and I want to meet you!"

Way 5 Do a mailing – but make it relevant

A little reminder in the mail never did any harm. You have a list of your clients and prospects? It's clean and up to date, with no duplications or silliness (dead people/fired people/gross errors)? When did you last do a general mailing to them? If it's over six months ago, maybe it's time to do another. What will you mail? Tell them some *news* about you, but make it relevant to their *needs*.

Some years ago, in the US, I wanted to run a mailing with the owners of Mooney aeroplanes – private four-seater "aerial Ferraris". Since aircraft ownership is all recorded, coming up with a list of the 4500 people involved was easy. But how could we get them to open the envelope? Well, every Mooney owner knows who Roy Lopresti is – he revolutionised the design of the Mooney a few years ago, and made it fly faster and smoother than ever before. So on the envelope, we put a slanting headline "Here's news about Mooney from Roy Lopresti". Roy signed the letter inside. We offered, among other things, a video brochure on the new Mooneys for $30. We sold 650 tapes – a 14 per cent response! And three $120,000 aeroplanes were sold directly attributable to the mailing.

Way 6 Ask for a reply

One of my most successful mailing pieces includes a postcard with a *postage stamp* on it (not a reply-paid card). It also contains a duplicate of the mailing label I used on the outside envelope. This invites them to ask me to phone, to explain something about what I've sent them, or to tell me they're not interested. I get about a 15 per cent response.

A corporate capabilities
video for
Pilkington Glass

Aimed at the automotive industry

The 50th-anniversary
video for **British
Midland Airlines**

On a 16-screen Videowall

A historical archive video:
*"The Admission to the
Freedom of the
City of London of
HRH The Princess of Wales"*

A training video for
Bayer Aspirin AG

In German, Italian & Spanish

Two training videos
for **Top Shop**
store managers

"Visual Impact I & II"

A pair of sell-through
videos for **Visnews:**
"WHEELS — The Joy of Cars"
&
"WINGS — The Jet Age"

A special project for the
North American Market:

*"Your Guide to Antique
Shopping in Britain"*

An in-flight video
appeal for

"Project Dreamflight"

The 1987 AGM video
for
The Burton Group PLC

*"Successfully Managing
Change"*

Previous work includes
other corporate and
educational projects

Including an interactive videodisk
for the
California Aerospace Museum

Extract from a CV prepared to resemble a storyboard

Way 7 Run an advertisement – but get it right

This can be costly unless you get it exactly right. I ran a quarter-page ad for a video I produced – *Your Guide to Antique Shopping in Britain* – in the special antiques issue of *Country Life*, and sold only three tapes. When I was head of advertising for Merrill Lynch in Toronto, we ran a double-page ad in the *Globe and Mail* with a coupon offering any of 29 different pieces of investment information, and received hundreds of replies, opening dozens of accounts. And an analysis of the 29 boxes that had to be ticked to receive the appropriate information told us a lot about what investors' interests and concerns were at that time.

"Only half of my advertising is effective," said one corporate ad biggie. "The trouble is, I don't know which half!" My advice is, unless you can afford to run regular advertising with a consistent message, you'll find other techniques more effective. One little ad won't do.

☞ **Timothy Foster**

❏ **I'd like to see your work; please call me**

❏ **What do you mean "interactive computer-based client briefing and script development for fast, effective results?"**

   ❏ **Please explain**

   ❏ **Prove it!**

❏ **I'm not interested. Sorry, old chap.**

My name is _____

My telephone number is _____

Postcard which deserves a response

Way 8 Create a newsletter

Do you have enough activity to warrant a regular newsletter? One of my suppliers, computer dealer Amsys Technology Ltd, sends me one, and as a result I've visited their showroom five times. So far, I've spent over £500 there in three months. I've hired their services as a consultant in developing some software, and I've had some equipment repaired. We have a *relationship*. And I'm looking lustfully at the new models that have recently been introduced.

One of the miracles of the Internet is that it enables very low-cost production and distribution of communications materials such as:

- newsletters

- E-zines (electronic magazines)

- on-line versions of newspapers and magazines.

The simplest of these are the special-interest newsletters distributed by e-mail. These are usually free. Check some out before you embark on one of your own. To order, you send an e-mail to the publisher with specified instructions in the body of the message. Their computer processes your request automatically, responding to your e-mail address. Some examples (with message required and e-mail-order address) are:

- Business This Week (The Economist – a weekly capsule review of key stories). Message 'join economist-business' to: newscaster@postbox.co.uk

- CNET Digital Dispatch (weekly computer/Internet news). Message 'subscribe dispatch' to: listserv@dispatch.cnet.com

- The Internet Tourbus (biweekly Internet hints and site reviews). Message: 'SUBSCRIBE TOURBUS Your Name' to: listserv@listserv.aol.com

E-zines are usually multi-page Web-sites. See BT's Business Connections, issued monthly at: <http://www.businesscon-nections.bt.com>. For a list of over 2000 e-zines, searchable by subject keyword, check out <http //www.meer.net/~johnl/ e-zine-list/keywords>.

Way 9 Place an article about what you do

Perhaps you have an interesting enough story for an appropriate publication. When I made the video, *Your Guide to Antique Shopping in Britain,* I got myself interviewed by the editor of *World of Antiques.* This ended up as a two-page article in the magazine. It was all about why I did it, and went into the philosophy behind the programme. Then the story became part of the sales presentation, to show the retailers the coverage we were getting. Later I placed an article in *Retirement Living* which was basically a modification of the video's script. We offered the tape in a sidebar and sold dozens.

Way 10 Get reviews of what you do

Somebody does something, and there's always somebody else to express an opinion. If you're in the right sort of field, seek out opportunities for people to review your activities – assuming you're proud of them! In my case, a review of one of my books, *The Aircraft Owner's Handbook,* became part of my advertising programme. *Aviation Consumer* – a sort of American private pilot's *Which?* magazine – reviewed it in these words: "With this book, the Library of Congress can close the doors to the general aviation stacks, because it's all there in eight vast codices unlike anything we've ever seen." *Art and Auction,* a US magazine, said of the antiques video: "A must for anyone who wants to try their hand at treasure hunting in the UK ... this video cassette is required watching." *That* went on the wrapper.

But maybe you don't write books or make videos. So what kind of review can you get? Look at the trade press for your industry. Don't they review products? *Flying* magazine reviews aeroplanes, and all the stuff that goes with them. Car books review cars. Camera books review cameras. *Campaign* reviews advertising. *PR Week* reviews PR campaigns. What do *you* do that can earn a review?

Then you make the reviews part of your programme. They go into your mailings, into your handouts, whatever.

Way 11 Develop a brochure

A brochure is designed to represent the product or service until it has been acquired or employed. It is there to help reinforce or replace personal experience. It needs to describe the *benefits* in glowing terms, creating desire. It should impart some of the same feelings as the real thing in an appetising way. It should ring of the same quality as the end product. (Not like the one I saw from a desk-top publishing agency offering 'Word Procesing'.) It should inform. It should be a reference point (including things like technical specifications, dimensions, addresses, phone and fax numbers, and so on). When your prospect or client wants action, the brochure should prompt a successful conclusion (business!). It should then become a hand-me-down, wending its way as an unsolicited testimonial into the arms of one of your clients' friends, along with a recommendation to use you or what you do. For practical advice on creating a brochure, see Way 62 in *101 Ways to Better Business Writing* (Kogan Page).

Way 12 Do a press release

Got something new to report? Will your trade press cover it? Then maybe a press release is the answer. No more than two or three pages of double-spaced typing, with a compelling headline and introduction, accompanied perhaps by a photo. Make sure the photo has a caption, and that the press release has a contact point (names, phone and fax numbers). Your objective is to get some link that can become the basis for further contact. Maybe the release will prompt a call from the publication asking for more information.

However, people who get press releases get perhaps 20 or more a day. So don't expect yours to be read all the way through in the first instance. First, you've got to get their attention! Your headline and the opening paragraph are the most important words on the paper.

Think about what kind of story the publication is looking for. Does your release sing this out? It has to. For practical advice on creating a press release, see Way 70 in *101 Ways to Better Business Writing* (Kogan Page).

Press Release

New Video Shows How to Shop for Antiques in Britain – by the People who Know.

London, March 1 1989: *Your Guide to Antique Shopping in Britain* – a new information programme on videocassette aimed at antique collectors, both experienced and new – was announced today. It is a one hour-long show, featuring interviews with some of Britain's leading antique dealers, as well as many experts and specialists in the field. It is hosted by well-known opera singer and broadcaster Nigel Douglas.

The programme concentrates on the major antiques centers in Britain: **London**, **Bath**, the **Cotswolds** and **East Anglia**. It visits dealers in these areas who describe some of their offerings, from exquisite antique jewelry to beautiful Chinese porcelain; from fine Regency furniture pieces to gorgeous textiles to Toby jugs on a stall on Portobello Road. The programme also visits the important London fairs, especially the **Grosvenor House Antiques Fair**, and those at **Olympia** and **Chelsea**. And it contrasts a country auction with one in London, giving the viewer important advice on attending antique auctions, and tours a country market in Long Melford.

People interviewed include **Judith** and **Martin Miller**, who write the hugely successful annual *Miller's Antiques Price Guide*, **John Andrews**, author of *The Price Guide to British Antique Furniture*, editors of the British antiques press **David Coombs** (*Antique Collector*) and **Ivor Turnbull** (*Antiques Trade Gazette*), the heads of the **British Antique Dealers Association**, and the **London and Provincial Antique Dealers Association**, as well as other leaders in the field.

Background is also presented by experts on restorations, how to spot fakes and protect yourself against buying one, furniture price and fashion trends, and how to bargain.

First page of press release

15

Way 13 Create a press kit

In an attractive folder gather a variety of implements describing your act. A copy of your brochure. The latest press releases (make sure the old, out-of-date ones are pulled). Reprints of other articles. Photos. Diagrams, drawings, charts. Anything that brings your story to life and that can be a reference for an inquisitive journalist. Hand it out to appropriate members of the press. The strategy is to use the press as influencers of your real audience, your clients and prospects.

Way 14 Do a Filofax insert

Have you noticed that a lot of your business contacts use Filofaxes? Then why not produce a page or two that will fit in their Filofax giving useful information about you and your industry? In my case, I created a reference page on which the holder could enter the names and numbers of freelance video crew people. My name and numbers were prominently displayed under the headings of *Writers, Producers* and *Directors.* On the back I put the phone numbers of key TV industry organisations, so it would be even more helpful to users.

Way 15 Create a calendar or desk-top item

Amazingly enough, people still need calendars. The calendar industry knows this and offers all sorts of solutions. Can you produce one that's relevant to you and that acts as a constant reminder?

What do people need on their desks that could have your name and number on it? The advertising specialities people await your call. Coffee mugs? Coasters? Calculators? Mouse mats? Pens and pencils? Paper clip dispensers? Paperweights? Executive decision-maker spinners? There's got to be something relevant to what you do that would work effectively.

Way 16 Get listed in trade directories

I'm amazed at how effective this can be. Newcomers and outsiders often use directories as their primary reference when they seek a solution to a problem. I got a nice piece of business last year because I was in the *Broadcast Production Guide.*

FREELANCE VIDEO PEOPLE — LONDON AREA

Resource/Name	Phone	FAX	Mobile
CAMERA			
DIRECTORS			
Foster, Timothy R.V.	034284-2873	034284-3210	0836-520792
EDITORS			
LIGHTING			
MAKE UP			
PRODUCERS			
Foster, Timothy R.V.	034284-2873	034284-3210	0836-520792
PRODUCTION ASSISTANTS			
PROPS			
SOUND			
WRITERS			
Foster, Timothy R.V.	034284-2873	034284-3210	0836-520792

Page from Filofax insert

My IVCA (International Visual Communications Association) listing produced the speaking engagement that has culminated in this book. The Yellow Pages or Thomson Directory can be important, too. But make sure they list it right. Years ago there was a coffee bar in Toronto called The Bohemian Embassy. You got it – you had to look it up in the Yellow Pages under Embassies and Consulates.

Way 17 Have your own Web-site

It is impossible to gauge the size of the Internet, it's growing so fast. One figure suggests that the World Wide Web (WWW) has over 200 million pages of information. Nobody knows. It's like an interactive, searchable library where any page of millions of books can be found and accessed, in any sequence, with the click of a mouse button. Thus it can tell your story to the world, too.

The scope, variety, depth, breadth and accessibility of information has never before been available on such a scale. It is truly worldwide and available around the clock, mostly at no cost. It is changing the way we work, act and think. It is becoming almost universally embraced by business, education, government, industry and the public (eg 100 per cent of UK and USA schools and all UK public libraries are targeted for connection by 2000).

Types of information available

Just about anything that can be read, listed, discussed, explained, compared, reviewed, displayed graphically, observed, listened to or commented on is on the Internet and can be easily found, eg:

- Corporate information (eg, advertising and brochure material, competitor intelligence, background/history, jobs available, mission statement, policies, press releases, product descriptions, plans, pricing, availability).

- Directories, catalogues, listings of suppliers and sources, addresses, phone/fax numbers (eg, Yellow Pages or association listings).

- Financial and investment data (eg, stock market data, annual reports, analyses, credit reports).

- Government statistics (eg, census data).

- Historic and archive material.

- Magazine/newspaper articles (abstracts and full text).

- Maps (from global to local street maps, subway lines, route maps).

- News (up-to-the-minute and previous reports).

- On-line databases (eg, movie cast lists, filmographies, discographies, books/authors/subjects, property available).

- Opinion, comment and information exchange on any subject.

- Personal subjects (eg, collecting, entertainment, food, hobbies, medical, pets, religion, special interests).

- Pictures and graphic images, charts, diagrams.

- Reference material (eg, how to apply for a new passport, visa requirements, tax information, patents, planning permission).

- Software (samples and for purchase).

- Travel information, rates, schedules (with reservation and booking capabilities).

A little time spent browsing the Web will soon give you ideas of what you can do with your own Web site.

Finding your way

Getting information from the Internet can be easy and swift or difficult and slow. It boils down to knowing where and how to look. You may have seen an advertisement or an article giving a Web site address (two thirds of trade magazine ads list one). That's a good place to start.

Your browser has a 'bookmark' feature which stores the URL (uniform resource locator) of a Web site you want to return to, so you can build a file of sites you want to visit often.

The first question to ask when seeking information is: What is my source – a bookmarked or known site or somewhere else? If it's bookmarked or known, just go direct. If the answer is somewhere else, then the question is: Do I know the site I need, but not the URL, or must I find an appropriate site? Then you use a search engine or try a link from a known Web site.

Understanding links

Links take you from the Web page you are on to the location selected. Links may come from screen buttons or <u>underlined text</u>. Many sites provide a page of links to sites of related interest which often give you the information you seek. Simply clicking on the link takes you there. If it turns out to be useful or interesting, bookmark it for easy future contact.

One of your most important tasks when you have your own Web site is to develop links from other relevant sites, see <http: //www.fonesave.com/websave/freeadtech.htm> for ways to do this. The latest trend is the 'Web ring', which is sort of a circular array of Web sites of similar interest linked together. If you're browsing a Web ring, you can go around it in either direction or at random. It is very easy to get your own Web site plugged into a ring. See <http: //www.venturetheweb.com/webring.html> for more information and <http: //www.webring.com> for a directory of Web rings.

Using search engines

These take your search parameters and, amazingly quickly – a few seconds – return links to Web sites that include them. Search by one or more key words.

The main engines, in ascending order of sophistication, are:

- Yahoo! <http: //www.yahoo.com> also <http: // www.yahoo.co.uk>
  - Broad general search of key words in Web-site *titles*; lets you search by category, eg, UK newspapers or Mexican hotels.

- Alta Vista <http: //www.altavista.digital.com>

- Broad general search of key words in Web-site *content*, not just titles; huge resource with over 60 gigabytes of information.

● Excite <http: //www.excite.com>

- Checks Web-sites, news articles from over 300 Web-based publications, data on thousands of cities worldwide, discussion postings in Usenet newsgroups.

● Britannica Internet Guide <http: //www.ebig.com>

- Pre-screened by Encyclopedia Britannica editors: classifies, rates, and reviews more than 65,000 Web-sites to give you the best of the best. Excellent.

Parallel searchers check a number of basic engines simultaneously, cut out duplications, then manipulate presentation of the results:

● Inference Find <http: //www.inference.com/ifind>

- calls out in parallel the best six search engines, merges the results, removes redundancies, and clusters the results into neat understandable groupings. Excellent.

How can you ignore a resource like this? Get on the Web!

Way 18 Join a relevant club

Where do your kind of business people hang out? Maybe there's a club or other establishment (pub? restaurant? bar?) where the clan gathers. Regular attendance may be hazardous to your health, but it can also help to oil the way to further, more businesslike meetings.

Way 19 Join a relevant trade association

For people in video production, it's the International Visual Communications Association. You get a listing in their directory, a certificate, membership benefits, a magazine and attendance at meetings where you can be a speaker and network to your heart's content. Consider standing as an officer. It could give you more clout.

Way 20 Be someone in the community

There are plenty of community activities that could make use of your services. When I lived in the US I became the PR adviser to a community action group that was fighting a nasty sewage-treatment plant proposal (nasty for us – it was to be upwind of our back gardens). Each week I attended meetings with the local community leaders, expanding my personal network the while. (We won, too.)

Way 21 Be famous for something else

What happens to old boxing champions in the US? They become greeters at Caesar's Palace in Las Vegas. Retired sports stars become car/insurance salesmen or stockbrokers. Record-breaking runners become news readers. Is there something in your past you can cash in on? Were you a child star? Or in your present? Are you an ace amateur athlete? What fame or notoriety do you have that you can put to use?

Many years ago, in what seems like a previous incarnation, I was the author of the only Canadian pilot's instrument rating training course. I became very well known in Canadian aeronautical circles. Then I joined Merrill Lynch as a stockbroker. Fresh out of the seven-month training programme, I sent out my first prospect mailing to a list of pilots. My letter started out "Dear Fellow Pilot: You may know me as the author of ..." Naturally, the mailing included a reply-paid folder to engender response. Soon, I received my first one back in the mail. With shaking hands I opened it. Here is what was written inside: "It is only because you are a fellow pilot that I have chosen to break these long years of silence, (signed) Amelia Earhart." And she didn't even give me her address!

How to Keep in Touch

What's the biggest problem facing you when you are looking for new business opportunities?

A Identifying prospects?
B Getting appointments?
C Conducting the interview?
D None of the above?

I suggest the answer is D.

It's building and maintaining a relationship.

And it starts with handling the response to the following line: "Well, that's very interesting. Thanks for dropping in. I don't have anything for you right now, but do *keep in touch.*"

Knowing how to keep in touch (KIT) and how to care for and feed your clients is one of the most important activities in your business dealings.

It's a well-known fact that many sales are not completed on the first call. It's not so well known that many sales are not completed until the *thirteenth* call.

So this section is about giving good KIT.

Way 22 Lend your prospect something that must be returned

When I was screening excerpts from videos I had created, with the head of in-house video at a major bank, the prospect became very interested in one tape: *Your Guide to Antique Shopping in Britain*. He was fascinated with the subject of antiques and wanted to see more. The programme is an hour long.

"Would you like to borrow it?" I said. Later, I called back to thank him for returning the tape and asked him how he enjoyed it. "You loved it? Great! By the way ..."

Way 23 Call before or after hours to bypass the secretary/PA

If they start work at 9 am, call your prospect at 8.30. If they leave at 5.30, call your prospect at 6 pm. Chances are he'll answer his own phone.

Way 24 Get your prospect's personal direct number and use it, but don't abuse it

If you are dealing with a big enough shot, he may have a direct telephone on his desk, that bypasses the company switchboard. The idea on incoming calls is that only he answers it. So if it's you on the other end, you'd better have a good reason to call. A simple KIT call ain't good enough. He'll have the number changed!

Way 25 Get to know the secretary/PA very well

A good secretary/PA is worth her weight in gold. And a good secretary/PA is worth *his* weight in gold. Whatever. They are interesting people who should be cultivated. Find out when their birthday is and send them a card. Bring in flowers to acknowledge special treatment. Make them your partner in dealing with their boss. *KIT* them!

I always make a point of getting the secretary/PA's name on initial contact. Then in my personal telephone listings and prospect databases I always list the PA's name right along with the target's.

Way 26 Leave a compelling message to ensure a call back

Unless you are a really important person, a totally fascinating conversationalist, or a really good friend, it's sometimes hard to penetrate the secretary/personal assistant/switchboard barrier if you're just calling to KIT. This is especially true if your prospect is "in a meeting" or "on the other line". How can you make him or her call back? Less than 20 per cent of people return calls to people like us (I made that statistic up, but it sounds right, doesn't it?).

When you are asked to leave a message, as well as your name and number, leave a subject that will trigger a response. You may even leave a deadline. "Please tell her I need her input for this article I'm writing for an important publication on what she does, and I'm on deadline, so I need to hear from her before 4 o'clock."

Way 27 Develop a reason to call back

Every KIT communication should evolve into an ongoing dialogue that continues over the days, weeks and months. So you need to derive a reason for the prospect to *want* you to call back, so that they are *expecting your call*, and leave strict instructions to be *interrupted* when you call, because it's *that* important. It could be the date of an event, a telephone number, the name of a book, the name of a product, the dealer who sells it, the reaction of a friend who uses it – something that only you can supply, that they want, but that you have to get back to them on. The trick is to do this every time, so there's *always* a reason to take your call.

Way 28 Never assume

If involved in a communication, never assume that it got through just because you sent it. This is especially true of faxes. Sending a fax does not mean receiving a fax. I once sent one to a client on a tight deadline on a weekend. After three hours he hadn't called back with his comments, so I phoned him. He said, "Where the hell is it? I've been waiting!" It turned out I had the wrong number. What's even worse is that the wrong number was also a fax, and on the following

Monday we got a fax from some mystery company wondering what this strange fax was all about.

When you *assume*, it makes an *ass* out of *u* and *me*.

Way 29 Remember, it's a numbers game

When I was in charge of sales training at Merrill Lynch in Toronto, I started a programme where we rewarded new brokers for making phone calls rather than for getting business. We knew that if you made 100 calls, you would get to see three people. If you saw three people, you would open two accounts. A year later, one of those would still be a good customer. The problem was that making a lot of phone calls and getting nowhere was demoralising. The constant rejection was hard to take. But by changing the dynamic to one where the job was to make calls, not to open accounts, it became much easier for them. And sure enough, when they opened an account, it was like a bonus. It made them feel good, and this had a positive effect on the way they worked; soon they were opening four accounts for every 100 calls. So when you are in KIT mode, and you can't get through, not no how, put a notch on your phone and dial the next number.

Way 30 If you just can't get through, lighten up

Let's say you want to KIT this prospect, and he just won't return your calls. Ten times out of ten. You've tried everything. You've called at 8 am, you've called at 6 pm, you've faxed him with the purpose of your call. It isn't very difficult to get yourself into a mode of outrage at the churlish treatment you're receiving. You start thinking of calling his boss and complaining (surely he'll return your calls then? You bet – right out the window!). You start leaving sarcastic – even rude – messages. Well here's some sound advice. Forget him. He's not worth your time. Put a notch on your phone and dial the next number. Strike him off your list. That way you win. Consign him to the loser's tip. Only winners get to deal with *you!*

Way 31 Ask questions

Don't be on *send* all the time. Sometimes you have to switch to *receive*. You must gauge the conversation and track it in the direction it's going. One time, we went on a new business pitch, which included a capabilities presentation on slides. There were three of us, all big shots. We sat down in the conference room, had a cup of coffee, made the small talk, and very soon the prospect started pouring his heart out on the table. It didn't take very long to get an idea of what he wanted, and we started talking about how we could address these needs. The meeting went on for over an hour, and the prospect started to get restless, so we began making moves to leave. "But wait," said one of my colleagues, "we haven't shown the slides!"

The point is, we were past the slides stage and into the meat of the discussion. Don't try to get yourself back on a track you don't need to be on any more.

Way 32 Get out of the office

Meetings on neutral ground allow you to focus on the relationship. Interruptions are cut out and you can concentrate on your objectives. Go for a stroll around the park, have lunch in a restaurant or club, meet for coffee in a hotel lounge, or even for a drink in a bar or pub.

Way 33 Be an extremely good joke teller

If you gauge that your prospect has a ready sense of humour, and you are an extremely good teller of jokes, try a few in an early meeting. If the prospect falls to the floor with uncontrollable delight, tell him you have more where that came from, but you are a little pressed for time right now, so you'll get back to him. As you review your e-mails you'll find lots of jokes people send you. You can develop an e-mailing list of buddies to share the good ones with (edit out the weak ones). Make sure they have a GSOH (good sense of humour) (grin). Only send jokes that will make them LOL (laugh out loud). But send each message personally addressed as an individual e-mail rather than broadcasting the message to 20 or 30 names. You don't want to disclose your list to everyone else, do you? Some people don't like that. Make sure you put a relevant subject in the header, perhaps with a: ☺ .

Here's an example:

SUBJECT: Q&As

Q What happened to the dyslexic Satanist?
A He sold his soul to Santa

Q How do crazy people go through the forest?
A They take the psycho path.

Q What do Eskimos get from sitting on the ice too long?
A Polaroids.

Q What do prisoners use to call each other?
A Cell phones.

Q What do the letters D.N.A. stand for?
A National Dyslexics Association.

Q What do you call a boomerang that doesn't work?
A A stick.

Q What do you call Santa's helpers?
A Subordinate Clauses.

Q What do you get when you cross an elephant and a skin doctor?
A A pachydermatologist.

Q What is a zebra?
A 25 sizes larger than an 'A' bra.

Q Why do bagpipers walk when they play?
A They're trying to get away from the noise.

Way 34 Get a biorhythm* calculator and use it

People are often reluctant to give their age. But if you can tell them their biorhythms, you'll get their date of birth, which

---

*The biorhythm theory is that there are three key cycles representing your intellectual (33 days), emotional (28 days) and physical (23 days) condition. In each cycle, you start out at neutral, go to a peak, back through neutral, down to a valley, then back up to the starting point. They are measured from the day you are born, and they go in and out of phase with each other throughout the year. When all three are at their peak, you are invincible. When all three are at their nadir, you will screw up. Today I'm 19,157 days old, and my biorhythms are Physical 21 (low, going up), Emotional 5 (high, about to peak) and Intellectual 17 (neutral, going down). I'll have a triple peak in one month's time, so watch out, world!

can be useful for other purposes (see Way 58). I had a pocket biorhythm calculator for years. It was the single most useful conversation piece I've ever had. I can remember, flying down to Washington with *Time* (see Way 53), having the chairman of the board of some big US company *kneeling* at my seat in the jet as I worked out his biorhythms! I also told him how many *days* old he was that day. It blew his mind! Now I have one on my computer. If you become the local biorhythm expert, people will call *you* for feedback. You can become important to them!

Way 35 Don't con your way on to the phone

When I was head of advertising at Merrill Lynch in New York, one day my phone rang and my secretary said, "It's the State Police!" Dropping everything, I raced for the phone, mentally going through what transgression I could have committed (I was an alien, after all). I picked up the phone: "This is Tim Foster."

"Hi there, Mr Foster, this is Sergeant Kendrick of the Florida State Po-lice." (Florida? I hadn't been to Florida for years!)

"Yes?"

"We'd sure like for you to buy some advertising in our State Po-lice Year Book. A page is just $300 ..."

I know some women who need to cold call top executives. They're speaking to the PA: "It's Miranda calling. No, just tell him Miranda . . . *He'll* know."

Of course, you could make it part of your business strategy to get past the PA in this way. What if you called your organisation the National Credit Agency, or the Bank? "It's the Bank calling . . . " Or the Clinic!

You may get through, but that's probably all you'll get.

How to Build Credibility for Yourself

The only way to build credibility for what you offer is to make every experience of dealing with you positive and unforgettable. You want to make sure your proposition works! It must be bomb-proof.

You must do things like delivering on, or ahead of, deadline. You must always exceed expectations. You should reinforce the positive reactions, and don't even let a negative reaction occur, but if it does, fix it and fix it fast!

It is the accumulation of experiences that establishes a primary image of credibility for you in the mind of your target. The image you establish will help to induce further experience of your products and services. Or it won't.

You want them to say of you: "You know, they're pretty good. They are a perfect example of the kind of thing we need in this area. There should be more like them."

You should be the second most informed person about the client's business (they're the first).

Way 36 Give him some intelligence

As you move through *your* world, be mindful of your *prospect's* world. If you hear something that your prospect's competitor is doing, call him up or send him an e-mail as below and tell him about it. Make sure you have your facts right. "Did you see that SoSo-FM has taken the billboard across from the railway station and they're broadcasting from it?"

Way 37 Fax her a press cutting or a note

When you see a story that would be important or interesting to your prospect in today's paper or the latest issue of an important magazine, fax it to her immediately, with a personal note. You are thinking of her needs and will be remembered.

What did we do before faxes were invented? Some of your contacts have their own fax sitting right near their office. Use that, rather than the big one in the mail room. A fax here and there that's relevant and interesting will do a good KIT job. But don't send 17-page faxes unsolicited! You'll be hated. Just KISS (keep it simple, stupid).

And now we have the Internet. As you review information on the Web, be mindful of little squibs of data that come up. If you see something of interest to a client, copy it into an e-mail and zap it to her. Include the Web site's address (the http://www stuff) if you can. Your intelligence will be appreciated. In fact any time you come across an interesting site, pass it on to those who would benefit. Let me give you one. Want medical information? Try <http://www.mediconsult.com>.

Way 38 Develop a project needing input from the prospect

I was invited to make a speech to the Writers' Group of the International Visual Communications Association (IVCA) of which I'm a member. Most of my prospects are also members. When I needed some background information for the speech, I contacted several of my prospects to get their input, and used it in the speech. (It was about keeping in touch . . .) People like to be considered as experts and to offer their advice. "I'm doing this speech to the IVCA tonight, and I'd like your advice. By the way . . . "

Way 39 Feed the results of the project back to them and others

I gave the speech (Way 38) and saw an opportunity to turn it into an article in *The IVCA Magazine*. (The editor was at the meeting, pleading with the audience for contributions, so I offered to do one based on tonight's speech. It was readily accepted.)

When the story appeared, I sent photocopies to the prospects who had helped, with a note: "Thank you for your contribution to this speech. By the way . . . " I also sent photocopies of the story to my other prospects with a note: "I thought you might be interested in this article of mine that recently appeared in *The IVCA Magazine*. By the way . . . "

Way 40 Identify a person you know that the prospect wants to meet and invite them both to lunch

If you are a good networking person, your conversation will get on to mutual acquaintances and contacts. It turns out that your prospect wants to meet a person you know. You be the *connector* and, if you're really broke, you can say: "Let me introduce you to Charlie. How would you like me to bring him round for lunch at your club?"

Being a connector is a very important part of what must be your ongoing networking activity. You become known as the person who can make useful introductions. In so doing you become a valuable contact for *your* contacts, and they'll be asking *you* for help.

Way 41 Develop a research programme

Create a research project. It's amazing how valuable this concept can be. In order to obtain the findings, you need to talk to your prospects. So what's the research about? It should be relevant to the industry you work in or that your prospects work in. What would people like to know about that industry? What findings would drive a good *story*?

A training company might want to know how its customers allocate their training resources. An airline might want to know how many trips their best customers take a year. A car dealership might want to know what their customers think of its service. A publisher of children's books might want to know about children's reading skills.

You then contact your prospects to interview them for the research and promise to get back to them with the results later – another reason to call. The results can then be turned into an article, which you can reprint and circulate to your prospects. If it's significant enough information, you can become identified with the research, and thus be an expert that people want to quote or interview on television.

As an exercise, look through the pages of a quality daily newspaper, and see if you can identify the stories that started out as the result of someone doing some research. I bet you'll be impressed.

Way 42 Invite your prospects over and make a presentation

Now you've done your research, turn it into a report, with slides or overhead transparencies. Contact your prospects and invite them to attend. Invite the press. The trade publications may well be interested in sending a journalist. You could arrange an interview so they can develop the story. Suggest interviews with one or two of your prospects, if relevant. Be the *connector*.

Way 43 Get interviewed on the radio or TV

On what programmes would a chat with you be interesting? Local programmes? Magazine programmes? Business programmes? You name it. Contact the news directors, producers or programme managers of the stations on your target list and suggest the idea. I did all kinds of radio interviews, some over the phone, some live, for my antiques video. In my case, we always offered their listeners one free tape, which helped to get us aired. (There are public relations consultants who can get you this kind of placement.)

When I was at Merrill Lynch, we employed my good friend Ann Benson to present a series of seminars around the US on investment know-how for women. Ann would always precede her seminar with pre-arranged appearances on afternoon local TV and radio chat shows. She was so credible and full of knowledge that she would often cause major phone problems downtown when they gave out the number of the local Merrill Lynch office to let people arrange to attend her talks. That was almost 20 years ago, and she's still doing it, to great effect.

Way 44 Take advantage of the interview to KIT

One interview I did live was on Radio Sussex, in Brighton. Coming up that weekend was the Brighton Antiques Fair, run by Caroline Penman. She's a good customer of mine and sells a lot of my tapes. As I started driving down to Brighton, an idea hit me. I called her on my car phone and said I was going to appear on Radio Sussex in an hour. I would mention her fair, so could she (a) give me some free tickets to offer over the air, and (b) offer a discount on my tape to anyone who mentioned hearing about it on the show? Of course. Caroline dropped everything and she and I met somewhere en route 30 minutes later in our matching Mercedes estates, as I made my way to Brighton for the live programme. She handed over the tickets and off I went to play boy broadcaster. Talk about a KIT exercise!

Way 45 Go for an award

Many professions and occupations have awards programmes. Perhaps you could enter some of your work. The trouble is this can get a little expensive. They usually want an entry fee of £100 or so. Hint: neatness counts. There's no doubt that winning an award enhances your stature. And it gives you something to put in your reception area or hang on your office wall.

Way 46 Become an awards judge

As you become elevated within your profession, it shouldn't be too difficult to become one of those erudite people who sit in judgement on an awards event. You'll at least be written up in the Awards Banquet Programme. It's also a good way of getting up to speed on what's being done in your industry. ("They think *this* is an award winner?!!")

Way 47 Become a trainer

If you are regarded as a bit of an expert in your field, perhaps it is appropriate for you to share some of your knowledge and ideas. In what situations could you impart this? In adult education? In courses for your clients' junior employees? On MBA courses? In courses you develop and organise yourself? As a supplier? A little research might pay off. You'll expand your own knowledge (the best way to learn something is to teach it), serve your fellow human beings and maybe even make a bit of money, to boot!

Way 48 Be part of the solution, not part of the problem

Cable News Network's Ted Turner has a sign on his desk: *Lead, Follow, Or Get Out Of The Way!* When you are part of the solution, people want to talk to you. When you are part of the problem, they want you to go away. Of which do you want to be a part?

How do you find out? Ask yourself this question: "Am I part of the solution, or am I part of the problem?" Then act accordingly.

Way 49 Solve problems intelligently

Don't say, "I really have to talk to him urgently, could you put me through?" This will get you, "I'm sorry, he's not taking any calls." Instead, say, "I really need to talk to him urgently. What would be the best way for me do that?" "He should be free in half an hour, can I get him on the phone for you then?" The barrier becomes your partner in helping you solve the problem.

Real-life example: I went into a pub ten minutes before afternoon closing time with my wife and two small children, starving after a morning of househunting. "Lunch for four, please," I said.

"We don't serve lunches after 2.30, the kitchen is closed," she said.

"How could I get something to eat for my family right now?" I said.

"I could make you up some sandwiches!"

"Done!"

You change the dynamic and you get what you want.

The rule is simple. You say "What do I have to do to get this done?" and doors will open for you as you have never experienced before. Promise.

Way 50 Offer to help them do their job

If she's doing a report of some kind, offer to provide input. This could enhance her interest in what you do or help her to clarify the need for your product or service. Or offer to review the report to serve as a sounding board before it's finalised. Your input could be in some area of expertise in which you specialise. It could be statistics, a quote on market conditions, or a chunk of one of your own documents. Ideally, you would like attribution, in which case make sure they get it right (right name, right company, right dates, etc). This is a freebie. Don't expect to charge for this, unless it feels right.

How to Grow the Relationship

Which would you rather be, a supplier or a business partner to your clients? Do you want to be challenged on price ("We can get it cheaper elsewhere"), or do you want to offer an added value that can't be obtained anywhere else? Do you want to take orders, or develop work based upon your advice and mutual understanding?

I think I know the answer.

So the answer to the question raised by the answer is that you must build and grow good relationships with your clientele.

It's like building and growing any living thing. It takes care and feeding, understanding and love. You plant the seeds at the right time. You water them and give them the right balance of light and shade. And you talk to them. Sometimes you may have to rush over and apply special treatment. But careful nurturing will produce prize-winning results.

And carelessness will produce disaster.

Here beginneth 27 ways to go about this *carefully*.

Way 51 Identify a personal interest

If you're in the person's office, look around at the pictures, plaques and knick-knacks. People like to have their stuff with them to remind them what they're working for.

It might be:

- A photo of our hero in front of his aeroplane, at the tiller of his boat, sitting on her horse, walking through Montmartre, being a magician, playing a sport, on skis, in a restaurant, standing in front of the Pyramids, shaking hands with the Duke of Edinburgh . . .

- A plaque or certificate honouring some achievement or contribution to society, a membership, a qualification, a milestone (100,000 miles flown on American Airlines, a hole in one) . . .

- A model of something to do with a pet hobby

- A trophy, even books on the shelves.

Select one that you know about and direct the conversation that way: "Are you a pilot? So am I . . . Where do you fly?"

From then on your contacts can revolve primarily around your shared interest. Work is merely incidental.

Way 52 How to address personal interests

The prospect in Way 22 is fascinated with antiques. So I addressed his interest. Since I made the video programme on antiques, I still get invitations to antique fairs and such. I sent him a spare one, with a personal note: "Thought you might be interested in this . . . "

Watch your mail. You may receive something that seems innocuous and boring to you, but it may really turn a client on who's interested in the subject. So pass it on.

Your prospect is interested in jazz. Go to lunch where they have a live band. He's a golf nut. Set up a foursome. She loves to ride. Get her tickets to the horse show. Etc.

Way 53 Invite your prospect to a special event

Theatre, concert or sporting event tickets. An invitation to a private screening. Dinner. An outing in the country. The Farnborough Air Show. Whatever turns him on. When I was at Merrill Lynch in New York, nobody did this sort of thing better than *Time* magazine. I was flown down to Washington to meet their Capital Bureau correspondents (in their company jet, after being picked up at my Manhattan apartment in a stretch limo). I saw *Jaws* three days before it hit the street. They invited me to be an expert speaker on a panel. I always returned *their* calls.

Way 54 Make your prospect special

In the rare event of your prospect coming to your office to meet you, make sure she feels welcome. Put her name on a welcome sign in Reception. But do it right. Years ago, some executives of Pepsi Cola went to an advertising agency to receive a pitch for their huge account. The receptionist said: "Let me take your coats, gentlemen. Mr Farnsbee will be out in a moment. Can I get you a Coke while you're waiting?" Uh, oh.

Way 55 Invite your prospect to speak at a function

If you're networking properly, you'll be involved in events where people make speeches. Perhaps your prospect has comething to say that would be interesting to your audience. You make him a star for a little while, maybe he'll make *you* a star!

Way 56 Invite your prospect to write an article

Perhaps you're involved in a publication – as an occasional contributor, a columnist, or maybe you just know the editor. Would it be helpful to your prospect's cause to pen a few words in your rag?

Way 57 Ask for his help with your pet charity

Maybe your prospect's company could help – the supply of product, use of facilities, lending of people or other resources, all these could become useful to your charity work. Working together on this type of project can bring you closer together.

Way 58 Send her a birthday card

Now you know her birthday (see Way 34), send her a birthday card. What's really amazing is how many people end up having the same birthday as you. This then becomes a special cause for celebration.

Way 59 Give them a lead

Your prospect may very well have to do what you do – sell a product or service – with a different audience (I sell the idea that I should write a video script for a producer, the producer sells it to his client as part of the overall production package, the client uses the video to sell his product to his customers). My prospect is the production company. Would it be a good career move for me to introduce the production company to another client? You bet it would. And I get the work that results.

Way 60 Invest in the company

If it's a public company, and the prospects look good, a modest investment might be an idea. You could talk to your contact within the company about whether he thinks it would be a good move. Does he invest in it? Ask him to have his people send you an annual report. (But don't ask for inside information!)

Back at Merrill Lynch, I was having lunch with a good consultant, Gene Casey Jr, of King-Casey, who did our corporate identity. "Did you see our latest earnings report? Pretty fantastic, huh?" I said. "Yeah! I'm a shareholder, you know," he replied. I didn't. "I make it a policy always to invest in my clients. I only like to have clients I would invest in!" That made *me* feel good. And *I* was the client.

Way 61 Phone with an idea

"I've got an interesting idea I want to discuss." What could it be? Some way for his company to save money? Something that came up in a conversation that could affect him? A new way to tell his story?

Way 62 Ask for a press kit

As part of your background in learning more about the company, you might request their latest press kit. This will have all kinds of information that could help you to evolve better ways to serve them. If it's really bad, you might even offer some polite criticism.

Way 63 Ask to be on their mailing list

If they have a house magazine, a newsletter or other regular mailing, these could be useful sources of information to help you formulate solutions to their problems that only *you* can provide.

Way 64 Become a customer

Maybe what they do is what you want. You scratch their backs, perhaps they'll scratch yours. Call your contact and ask for her advice on placing the order (don't ask for a discount – let her offer it).

Way 65 Offer a gift, relevant to what you do, to induce response

In the newsletter example (Way 8), the reason I went to the showroom the first time was because they offered a free bit of software for my computer. It was a telephone area code reference that I could install in my computer and use at will. Tap in the city and it tells me the dialling code. Tap in the code and it tells me the city. Useful, and it demonstrates the dealer's programming skills.

Way 66 Get sponsored for charity

There's always some run or other event put on by a charity that's seeking participants who will get sponsorships. But make it *relevant!* Then invite your clients and prospects to sponsor *you*.

Way 67 Combine one client's activity with another client

You can take advantage of all kinds of things by combining activities between one or more other clients. Once again, you become the *connector*. You create a partnership between the clients and act as the go-between. Kodak Batteries had an exclusive at Toys R Us over Christmas that did a lot to load customers up with alkaline power cells. TDK audiotapes had a deal with Pizza Hut where you get a package of reductions on pizzas when you buy a five-pack of TDK cassettes. What kinds of deal can you come up with? Your call about one of these will probably not go unwelcome.

Way 68 Attend their industry trade shows and exhibitions

A good way to get up to speed on the state of the art in the industries you serve is to go to their trade shows. You may also get to *schmooze* (chat up, cater to, make feel important) the client at his stand. I once helped to make some videos for British Olivetti about their computers. I even appeared in a couple, as well as writing them. Later I attended the Computer Show at London's Earls Court, and there I was, on the big screen at the Olivetti stand! And there was the client, appreciating the personal visit. Strike up another KIT.

Way 69 Call to congratulate

Keep your eye on the press, especially in your industry. If something good happens involving your client or prospect, call up and share her joy. A promotion? An award? A good review? A successful product launch? Maybe you can help to extend this good news by doing what you do. Sending flowers isn't out of the question.

Way 70 Call to commiserate

When you keep your eye on the press, look not only for the good tidings. If your prospect is dealing with bad news, call up and share his misery. Maybe you have a way to help overcome the problem. A loss of a contract? Lay-offs? A decline in earnings? A crisis?

Way 71 Get well soon

Is your prospect off work and unwell? Possibly a card or flowers to the hospital would not go amiss.

Way 72 Send her a book

When you find a book that expresses your thinking well, and reflects on your unique selling proposition, give copies of it to your prospects. If you've written a book yourself, what could be a better gift, if it's at all relevant or interesting? I've written seven *101 Ways* books, so I've always got something to offer. If you haven't written a book yet, you're welcome to use some of mine! Here they are:

- *101 Ways to Succeed as an Independent Consultant*
- *101 Ways to Get More Business*
- *101 Ways to Generate Great Ideas*
- *101 Ways to Get Great Publicity*
- *101 Great Mission Statements*
- *101 Ways to Better Business Writing*
- *101 Ways to Boost Customer Satisfaction*

Way 73 Give them something you've done

A few years ago, I did a sell-through video called *Wheels – The Joy of Cars*. It became my Christmas present for my clients and prospects. Last year, I did the same thing with my video *Your Guide to Antique Shopping in Britain*. Next year, it'll be this book, if I haven't already given it to them in some other manner.

Way 74 Treat them to something special that you do

When I lived in the US some years ago, I had my own aeroplane, a beautiful four-seater Piper Comanche. Quite often I would fly in to see a prospect, ask him to meet me at the airport and end up taking him for a little ride. "Can I bring my kids?" You bet.

Way 75 Don't be afraid to ask for referrals or introductions

If you do have a good relationship, don't be afraid to ask for referral business. I am amazed at how many times I have asked for a referral, and got a very good one leading to good business, which would never have happened if I hadn't posed the question. There's an implied third-party endorsement that helps, too.

I developed a unique service called The Slogo Register. It's a database of advertising slogans. Ad agencies use it to check whether a proposed line has been used before. I usually turn around a search in about three hours (the agencies love this). Now whenever I work with a new client, after I've delivered my report (which I fax right from my Mac), I phone to make sure that they're satisfied and ask if I can e-mail a description of what we do (most agencies have e-mail these days) and could they circulate this to their colleagues, please? Always yes, often leading to repeat business from new people at the agency. Note that I strike when the iron is hot – at the moment of satisfaction. Most people are only too happy to recommend something they are impressed with to their associates.

Way 76 Give your best client's offspring a summer job

What better way to cement a trusting relationship than to put one of your client's teenagers to work one summer? This takes the art of KIT to its ultimate. Perhaps there's a project you want to finish that just can't seem to get done. Bring in the kid!

Way 77 Write a thank-you note for a piece of business

People remember the little courtesies. It's a fact, a good relationship with your client is more important than doing great work and having a lousy relationship.

How to Work with your Clients in the Development Stage

Notice I say work *with*, not work *for*. The aim is to be thought of as your client's partner or consultant, rather than someone who takes a brief and turns in a result.

By involving your clients in what you do, you build a sense of ownership. There is a lot of satisfaction to be had in working a problem through and coming up with a solution. It produces a valuable bonding that can't be obtained any other way.

At the very least, it has to do with keeping your client in the loop, asking for feedback as you go along, making mid-course corrections as necessary, asking for a reality check.

And all this contributes to building and maintaining that all-important *relationship*.

Way 78 Involve your client in the work

If you take a brief and go away and do all the work and come back and say "Here it is!" you put yourself in the position of being judged. Maybe there's something about it they don't like. Maybe they reject it. If you haven't involved them in the development, you're dead.

At least you should check in half-way through the activity and review your progress. This is as true if you are painting her living room as it is if you are developing a marketing communications programme. It's about *ownership*, of which more in a moment.

Way 79 Involve the *right* client in the work

Back in the US, I once created a slide show for a major client. I was given the brief by Mr Big, and was assigned Mabel Minion as my contact. In my dealings with Mabel, I got approval to all the slide copy (100 slides), and to the layout and basic design, which was very elegant and classy. I sent samples of the slides to Mabel before we went ahead and received an OK. Then we made the slides, and I flew up in my trusty Piper Comanche to present the show. It was beautiful. The last slide popped through and the lights went up. Then there was an extremely long and increasingly uncomfortable silence. I looked at Mr Big with an expectant smile on my face. "That's the worst slide show I've ever seen!" he snarled. Well, it seems he had this idea that slides should have **VERY BIG LETTERS** on them. Mabel had never shown our layouts to him. Now what? Well, we had done our part. I was happy to revise the slides (easy to do, thanks to computers), but he wouldn't let me. He redid them himself! But I still needed to get paid. And, after some uncomfortable months, I eventually did. But I never worked for that client again.

Lesson: *make sure the ultimate client is in the loop.* And keep that relationship going.

Way 80 Involve your client in the work – why

I said this is about ownership. If you have a major project to undertake, and you do it all on your own, without client involvement, who owns it when you walk in to show the result? You do. And now you have to sell it. All the clients sit in judgement. If one doesn't like it, she'll start trying to unsell it, so that she can be right. Who is your ally in the room?

Now if you had involved the client from the start, going back and forth, exchanging ideas, reaching agreement as you went along, who owns it when you go in to show the result? Your client-partner. He will sell it for you. You just sit back and nod. You have an ally because you are a *team*.

Way 81 Involve your client in the work – how to

I use my computer to good avail in involving my clients in my work. When I have to write a video script, after I've taken the brief, I'll develop a treatment, get agreement to this and then do the first draft of the script. Then we go into my unique "interactive computer-based script development mode". It works like this. I sit down with the client (maybe two or three people), with me at the computer keyboard, and they looking over my shoulders at the screen.

The computer's screen is WYSIWYG (what you see is what you get). This means that text that appears on the screen resembles a finished script printed on paper. **Boldfaced** words are **bold**. *Italics* are *italic*. The layout is right. We start going through the script, scene by scene, and I read the dialogue or commentary. I ask if the words sound right. I get them to read them and make changes. Thanks to the computer, if we don't like something, we can change it. It's not only effortless, the end product is a script, that looks like a script, that they *own*. And the whole process takes maybe two or three hours. I have used this technique dozens of times, and *it works!* I've also used it when writing a speech, with great success.

Way 82 Talk up the benefits, not the features

A lot of people have a problem with this in the early years of their careers. People don't buy products, they buy benefits. They don't buy a stereo, they buy "beautiful sound". They don't buy a video recorder, they buy "freedom to watch TV on their own terms".

I will now give you my secret for recognising a benefit from a feature, and for getting to the *ultimate benefit*. The ultimate benefit is the most compelling reason to buy, based on that specific feature.

My secret is based on the word *so*. All you do is make a statement about the product or service, and then say "so ...?" There needs to be a slight questioning inflection in your voice. And you keep saying "so ...?" until you get to the ultimate benefit.

For example: "This video recorder (VCR) has its own tuner, so ...? You can record a programme on one channel while you are watching one on another channel, so ...? You can run your life on your own terms, not on the dictates of a programme schedule, so ...? You can get more out of your time, and do what you want when you want, so ...? You can be free, so..." When you run out of responses to the word "so ...?", you should be at the ultimate benefit.

Way 83 Don't confuse process with result

There is a tendency for people to fall into the belief that they are doing their job if they are busy doing it. But what the client wants is a result. Process is incidental and not the desired answer to the question "How are we doing?"

Let me give you an example. In its first incarnation, I called this book *101 Ways to Further Yourself as an Independent Consultant*. When the publishers accepted it, their first suggestion was to entitle it *101 Ways to Succeed as an Independent Consultant*. Absolutely right. Get to the ultimate benefit – the result. You want to further yourself, so ...? You can be a success, so ...? You can do the things successful people do, while less successful people watch, so ...? All *right*, already!

Way 84 Understand your objectives and look at them frequently

It's easy to have a knee-jerk reaction to a stimulus, and go off in a direction that addresses an immediate problem that seems to have surfaced. But what are we trying to do here? People allow themselves to lose sight of their objectives when they get bogged down in detail.

It's not a bad idea to create a sign stating the key objective and hang it on the wall where you can see it while you work. If you find yourself wading through seemingly irrelevant activities on your way to the solution, stop for a moment and say: "Just a minute! What's the issue here? Why I am I doing this?" If you answer truthfully (to thine own self, etc.) you may find that you've got off track. This little exercise can help you to get back on.

Way 85 Know the difference between objectives and strategy

A lot of people get the concepts of objectives and strategy mixed up. An *objective* is simply what you want to achieve. Start all statements of objective in the infinitive, and make them *measurable*:

- To have my private pilot's licence in 12 months' time (not "To learn to fly").

A *strategy* is how you propose to achieve the objective. Start all statements of strategy with an active verb:

- Take flying lessons.

Another way of being clear about strategy is to link it to the objective with the word *by*, as follows:

- To have my pilot's licence in 12 months' time, by taking a good course of flying lessons from a reputable school.

Way 86 Let your strategy dictate your tactics

Once you're clear on what it is you want to achieve, and how you intend to go about it, develop a programme and stick with it. If what you do can be made to fall under the heading of your strategic statement, you're on strategy. If what you do demands its own heading, you are probably off strategy.

- Take flying lessons
  - Go to local airport and talk to flying school people

- Send off for literature from flight schools
- Establish budget and timetable
- Attend Paris Air Show (Is that on strategy?)
- Buy *Jane's All the World's Aircraft* (Is that on strategy?).

Way 87 "We're not ready to make a decision on this"

If you want to progress your proposal, you should try to identify what the *real* objection is. Questions like "What are the barriers to doing this?", "What do we have to do to get this off the ground, Wilbur?" will help. You may then find out what the real problem is. Maybe they have no money right now. Maybe they've just bought the same thing somewhere else. Maybe you haven't convinced them yet. "Are there any barriers to our doing this?" is another good question to ask.

If you can clearly identify an objection, you can address it. And you can't if you can't.

Some people have been trained not to make a decision until the last moment that they have to. This can be frustrating, because you're ready to go *now*. If you sense this is the case, give them a real deadline to work to, with supporting evidence. "I must know by Tuesday 10 am if you want this, because the firm deadline for submitting our tenders is 3 pm that day. We're ready to go if you are."

When they say yes, get on with it! As brokers at Merrill Lynch, we were trained to confirm the order, say thank you and *hang up!*

How to Work with your Clients in the Ongoing Stage

This section is about not taking your clients for granted. It's so easy to do. You get a new client, and they start taking more of your time. You think of your other clients – "Oh, they'll understand". But be wary! Predators are around, waiting to romance your old clients away from you with a little of the care and attention that you've been unintentionally withholding.

There was a rhythm and blues song a few years ago that said it well. The key lines were:

"Who's makin' love //
to your old lady //
while you're out makin' love?"

Way 88 Update her on your work

When did you last show your *existing* clients what you do? Maybe it's time to show some of your latest results. Too often the people that know us best are the people we spoke to yesterday. We tend to take our long-term clients for granted.

Way 89 Ask for feedback and evaluation

Don't be afraid to ask how you are doing. If there are any problems, it's better that you find them out early than receive a nasty phone call one day far in the future. Questions like: "Are you happy with this?", "Is there anything you're not happy with?" are the sorts of opener that could let you know if there are any problems.

Way 90 Involve their colleagues

One big danger in business relationships is that people move on. They change jobs, retire, get fired, die – all kinds of things. If your relationship is based on one person, start involving others if you can. Invite your client to bring colleagues into the picture, if only to help them understand more of what you do. Otherwise you could be in for a nasty surprise if your chief contact leaves. A new person might think that means they are a new broom.

I have an ongoing relationship with a large firm, and I do work for several people there. But there are lots of people I don't work with for whom I could. So I recently started a programme of expanding awareness of what I do among *them*. I was amazed. Here were all these people, that I knew, that I had never worked with, who somehow had no idea of how I could help them. There are all kinds of opportunities right under your nose. Just yesterday, I made such a presentation. There were three people in the room, only one of whom I knew. After 45 minutes, I walked out of the room with a good piece of business from a man I had never met, who until that moment had never heard of me. *Don't ignore the obvious!*

Way 91 Update your client on what's going on

When I was a stockbroker, I found that my clients liked to get calls telling them how their shares were doing. It could be simply to tell them today's prices, or perhaps to report on an announcement about the company that had come over the news wire. It shows you care.

Way 92 Update your client – even when the news is bad

Clients of stockbrokers may not like to get calls telling them how badly their shares are doing. But far better they should hear it from you – their trusted adviser – than on the evening stock market report as they drive home. Maybe you can evolve a containment strategy.

There's a saying in the City: "Cut your losses and let your profits ride". Many investors have a fear of selling a stock they've lost money on: "I don't want to take that kind of a loss – but we've got a nice profit on the other one, so let's sell that." The unfortunate thing about this strategy is that you end up with a portfolio of losers. Which do you think the client wants?

It's about giving tough advice. It may feel uncomfortable for you, but it is in the best interests of the client, and in the long run he'll thank you for it.

How to Work with your Clients when you Have Problems

Problems will not go away by themselves. They must be confronted and dealt with. If you don't control the handling of a problem, somebody else will, and it may thus not be to your client's or your own advantage.

It's very easy to procrastinate your way along a problem, but the sleepless nights that may result are probably not worth it.

Good questions are: "What is the issue here?", "What is the *real* problem?", "What do we have to do to solve it?"

If you have bad news for a client, far better you deliver it than let them find out the hard way – such as on TV or by reading the newspaper. In your role as partner and counsellor, dealing with problems is as much your responsibility as dealing with the good stuff.

One of my clients is in the business of training its clients to be interviewed by the press. The process is called *media training*. This is an intensely interactive process in which the clients are videotaped as they experience simulated interviews. Then the results are discussed and criticised. Further repeats show the improvement that the training achieves as the day goes on. One thing that has become clear is that media training improves the relationship. And if there are problems with the relationship, media training helps to deal with them and work them out. Is there a parallel in what you do?

Way 93 Phone him to give him criticism

There are probably a few things about this outfit you call a client that could stand improvement. Does their switchboard handle telephone calls well or do they let it ring, ring, ring for ever? When they mail out a brochure, does it feel as though someone cares, or is it redolent of a crummy mail room operation? Do they respond to their advertising leads promptly? Do they come out to service calls on time, or is it "He'll try to get there as soon as he can, hopefully"? How is the product when it comes out of the box? Does it work, or is it junk? So, if your relationship is on the up and up, perhaps some polite comment might be appropriate. If the relationship is precarious, you may want to treat this differently, however.

Way 94 Be a good loser

You've pitched for the business, made an outstanding proposal, you thought you had it in the bag, and at the last minute, the other man gets the job. Now what? The important thing is to maintain the relationship. Let things settle down a bit, then continue with a low-key contact programme. Sometimes the other guy will screw it up, and the prospect will need a fast bail-out. Or maybe their work just won't be good enough for a repeat, and you could get it next time. But you won't get much if you don't keep the relationship going.

Or you've been serving the client for some years, and it's time to renew the contract. Then he tells you they've decided to switch to one of your competitors. Having established you can't save the business, what do you do? Maintain the relationship with your key contact people. They're not going to return too many of your calls in the early days, but if they keep getting thoughtful little communiqués and the occasional lunch, you should be able to divine if there are any problems with the new outfit. Remarriages do happen.

Way 95 Why did you lose?

Should you find out why you lost the business? By all means. You should know if there's a problem, or if there's some other reason. Knowing this will help you to avoid similar problems in the future, or will show you that the reason was beyond your control (like "the boss wanted to do business with the other man because they went to school together").

Way 96 If you have a cash collection problem, deal with it

You really need to get this sort of thing out of the way. Find out what the problem is and negotiate a solution. If the relationship is important to you, how much are you prepared to spend to keep it? Or how much do you need to make to lose it? It might be costly to replace the client just to save your wounded pride.

Way 97 If you screw up, own up

"The best thing about telling the truth is you don't have to remember what you said." How do you handle the delicate situation where you really made a booboo, inconveniencing your client no end, and generally making your name mud? You own up and face up to it. No excuses. "I screwed it up. I'm terribly sorry to have inconvenienced you. How can I make amends?" This is why a good relationship is so important. Nobody suffers fools gladly, but everyone makes mistakes. If the relationship is there, you are allowed the occasional error.

Way 98 You have a great relationship, then your colleague harms it

This can happen all too often. You've spent months developing the relationship, and it's time to bring your colleague in to meet your prospect. And he completely ruins it. What happened? Did he get out of the wrong side of bed this morning? Has he been drinking? Is he on drugs? Is he crazy? Whatever the reason, here you are, with a great programme that you've worked out together with your contact, ready to go, and your own colleague firmly and convincingly smashes it to pieces. Talk about split loyalties!

Rule 1: Don't get into an argument with your colleague in front of the client.

Rule 2: Don't let your client get into an argument with your colleague in front of you.

The strategy here is damage containment. As quickly as possible, draw the meeting to a close, and get him out of there. Very soon thereafter, identify the problem areas and call your contact with an apology for what happened in the meeting and a promise to work things out. Then address and resolve the problem areas.

It's quite possible your colleague has killed this step of your programme's development. Your strategy must be, if you want to save the relationship, to start rebuilding again. It's almost back to square one. And that may be as true of your relationship with your colleague, too.

Way 99 You've worked out a great programme together, and their inside experts kill it

This just happened to me. I was working on a script for a training film for a bank, and in my initial meetings with the clients (training manager and product manager) had proposed a way to tell the story. The film was to introduce a refinement to one of their credit cards. We'd show a teller having a conversation with a customer in which she'd be asked to explain the new service, since the customer had read about it. The teller knows nothing and promises to get some information to give the customer on his next visit. She then asks a senior branch person about it. This person has just come off a training seminar and knows all. She wants to try out her new knowledge, so she and the teller agree to go through it together. Thus we convey the information, and the customer is then well served.

This idea was enthusiastically accepted and I went off and drafted version one of the script. Now came the interactive script-development session (see Way 81). The two happy clients were there, and for the first time, the experts from their in-house video production department. I thought we would simply be massaging my wonderful script, and turning it into a completely effective piece of training. How wrong I was. The experts started off: "This won't work. We've tried it before, and we find that staff don't like to see them-

selves portrayed in training films. They get uncomfortable."
The two clients looked at each other, and at me. Now what?

I stayed cool. I decided it would be a waste of time trying to
save the idea. "Let's see if we can come up with a solution," I
said. There and then, I ran a mini brainstorming session, and
pretty soon we evolved the idea of using a newscast format.
We'd have a professional reading the news, and we'd introduce the service as if it were tonight's hot story. Within two
hours, we had the bones of a script worked out, and the day
was saved.

Moral: Don't try to defend your work against their experts.
Address their needs. I did. I put them first and made it.

Way 100 Your client says, "Call me back in six months." Now what?

You've been working on some suggestions, you've had meetings, you've made proposals. The first reaction is, "It's nice,
but I want to check my budget. Let's see how the year starts
off, and take it from there." You go back some weeks later.
They don't return your calls. Finally, after the third call, the
PA comes back to you: "What did you want to discuss?" You
tell her. You ask for a meeting to progress the idea. Can she
work it out? You agree to call the PA back. You call back. "We
really don't have any money in the budget right now for this.
Can you call back in June?"

Unless you can come up with a different approach, what
you have to do here is maintain a low-key contact programme. Send clippings that reinforce your selling points.
Drop them a line in three months. Invite them to lunch one
day. You've got to keep the relationship going.

Putting It All Together

In this book we've looked at 100 ways to succeed as an independent consultant. (The 101st is on the next page.) We've looked at:

- How to promote what you do
- How to keep in touch
- How to build credibility for yourself
- How to grow the relationship
- How to work with your clients in the development stage
- How to work with your clients in the ongoing stage
- How to work with your clients when you have problems

Now we get to the punch line – how to put it all together.

The solution is to have a good understanding of the processes outlined here, and to know when to use them. I hope some of the ideas in here will prompt other ideas for you, based on your own experience.

So how do I put it all together?

Way 101 Write a book

You're holding mine in your hand. Did it help? I certainly hope so. Write and let me know (or e-mail me at fostair@atlas.co.uk):

Timothy R V Foster
c/o Kogan Page Limited
120 Pentonville Road
London N1 9JN

I do a stand-up piece at seminars called: *Write a book about what you do.* It is absolutely the best way to become an acknowledged leader in your area whom people seek out for advice! Here are the key points

Check the existing literature

Look at your line of business. What books are there out there now on the subject? You should have a reasonable awareness of this, but if you don't, visit a good library. Go to a couple of good bookshops and check out the scene.

Checklist for writing a book

To start, answer these questions:

- What is my objective?
- What is the working title?
- What is the sub-title?
- What is the book about?
- Who will buy it?
- What needs does it fill?
- What does the author bring to the party?
- What is the format (hardcover, paperback, etc)
- Who should publish it?

Assuming you can answer these, start working. Write the table of contents. Write single-paragraph descriptions of each chapter, and write at least one chapter.

Selling your book

Forget agents. They are mostly *useless* for this kind of work. I've never had an agent able to sell a trade book on my behalf. Most of them don't even want to look at what you do, because they're 'too busy'. Yet I've sold over twenty books on my own, working directly with publishers.

So write to your target publisher. If you don't know whom to contact, telephone and ask for the name of the person to write to, and send a one-page descriptive letter, with this information:

- The proposed title.
- The target audience.
- The rationale/need for the book.
- The chapter headings.
- How many pages you expect it to be.
- The style – paperback, coffee-table, etc.
- How many illustrations.
- When and how you can deliver it (floppy disk, paper, etc).
- Your price ideas.
- Your timetable.
- Your credentials as author – CV, copies of articles, etc.

You may not make a lot of money writing a book, but the mileage you can get out of it is worth all the aggro. If you do write a book as a result of this, please send me a copy (address as above), and I'll send you one of mine.

Useful Addresses – Associations and Organisations

Architects and Surveyors Institute
15 St Mary Street
Chippenham
Wilts SN15 3JN   01249 444505

Art Workers Guild
6 Queen Square
London WC1N 3AR   0171 837 3474

Association for Information Management, The (ASLIB)
Staple Hall,
Stone House Court,   0171 903 0000
London EC3A 7PB   http: //www.aslib.co.uk

Association for Management Education & Development
14–15 Belgrave Square   0171 235 3505
London SW1X 8PG   http: //www.management.org.uk

Association of Accounting Technicians
154 Clerkenwell Road   0171 837 8600
London EC1R 5AD   http: //www.aat.co.uk

Association of British Aviation Consultants
c/o Royal Aeronautical Society
4 Hamilton Place
London W1V 9FD   0171 499 3515

Association of Building Engineers
Jubilee House
Billing Brook Road
Weston Favell   01604 404121
Northampton NN3 8NW   http: //www.abe.org.uk/abe

Association of Business Executives
14 Worple Road
London SW19 4DD   0181 879 1973

Association of Consulting Engineers, The
12 Caxton Street   0171 222 6557
London SW1H 0QL   http: //www.acenet.co.uk

Association of Consulting Scientists
PO Box 4040
Thorpe-Le-Soken
Clacton on Sea
Essex CO16 0EL   01255 862526

Association of Illustrators
1st Floor 32–38 Saffron Hill
London EC1N 8FH   0171 831 7377

Association of Independent Computer Specialists, The
90 Deeds Grove
High Wycombe   0701 070 1118
Bucks HP12 3NZ   http: //www.aics.org.uk

Association of Independent Crop Consultants
Agriculture House
Station Road
Liss
Hants GU33 7AR   01730 895354

Association of MBAs
155 Duncan Terrace   0171 837 3375
London N1 8BZ   http: //www.mba.org.uk

Association of Noise Consultants
6 Trap Road
Royston
Herts SG8 0JE   01763 852958

Association of Photographers, The
9–10 Domingo Street
London   0171 608 1441
EC1Y 0TA   http: //www.photouk.co.uk/assop_txt.html

Better Business (formerly Home Run)
Cribau Mill
Llanvair Discoed   01291 641222
Chepstow NP6 6RD   http: //www.better-business.co.uk

British Association of Women Entrepreneurs
Kenwood House
114 Gloucester Place
London W1 3DB   0171 935 0085

British Institute of Professional Photography
Fox Talbot House
2 Amwell End
Ware
Herts SG12 9HN   01920 464011

Chartered Institute of Journalists
2 Dock Offices
Surrey Quays Road
London SE16 2XU   0171 252 1187

Chartered Institute of Marketing, The
Moor Hall
Cookham, Maidenhead   01628 427200
Berks SL6 9QH   http: //www.cim.co.uk

Chartered Society of Designers
1st Floor 32–38 Saffron Hill   0171 831 9777
London EC1N 8FH   http: //designwebb.co.uk

Composers Guild of Great Britain
The Penthouse
4 Brook Street
London W1Y 1AA   0171 629 0886

Direct Marketing Association
1 Oxendon Street   0171 321 2525
London SW1 4EE   http: //www.dma.org.uk

Federation of Small Businesses Ltd
32 Orchard Road
Lytham St Annes
Lancs FY8 1NY   01253 720911

Forum of Private Business
Ruskin Chambers
Drury Lane   01565 634467
Knutsford, Cheshire, WA16 6HA   http: //www.fpb.co.uk

Geologists Association
Burlington House
Piccadilly
London W1V 9AG   0171 434 9298

Guild of Aviation Artists
71 Bondway
London SW8 1SQ   0171 735 0634

Guild of Professional After Dinner Speakers
12 Little Bornes
Alleyn Park   0181 670 5585
London SE21 8SE   http: //www.ivorspencer.com

Home Aloners UK
Borlase
South Street
Blewbury   01235 851065
Oxfordshire OX11 9PX   http: //www.homealoners.co.uk

Incorporated Society of Musicians
10 Stratford Place   0171 629 4413
London W1N 9AE   http: //www.ism.org

Independent Financial Advisers Association, The
12–13 Henrietta Street   240 7878
London WC2E 8LH 0171   http: //www.ifaa.org.uk

Independent Safety Consultants Association
PO Box 5001
Redditch
Worcs B98 0RY   01527 52480

Institute of Chartered Secretaries and Administrators
16 Park Crescent   0171 580 4741
London W1N 4AH   http: //www.icsa.org.uk/icsa

Institute of Directors
116 Pall Mall
London SW1Y 5ED   0171 839 1233

Institute of Employment Consultants
3rd floor Steward House
16A Commercial Way
Woking   01483 766442
Surrey GU21 11ET   http: //www.iec.org.uk

Institute of Independent Business
Clarendon House
Bridle Path
Watford   01923 239543
Herts WD2 4AA   http: //www.iib.org.uk

Institute of Information Scientists
44 Museum Street
London WC1A 1LY   0171 831 8003

Institute of Linguists
Saxon House
48 Southwark Street   0171 940 3100
London SE1 1UN   http: //www.iol.org.uk

Institute of Management, The
Management House
Cottingham Road
Corby   01536 204222
Northants NN17 1TT   http: //www.inst-mgt.org.uk

Institute of Management Consultants
5th floor
32–33 Hatton Garden   0171 242 2140
London EC1N 8DL   http: //www.imc.co.uk

Institute of Management Services
1 Cecil Court
London Road
Enfield
Middx EN 2 6DD   0181 363 7452

Institute of Marine Engineers
76 Mark Lane   0171 481 8493
London EC3R 7JN   http: //www.imre.org.uk

Institute of Patentees and Inventors, The
Suite 505A, Triumph House
189 Regent Street   0171 434 1818
London W1R 7WF   http: //www.invent.org.uk

Institute of Personnel and Development, The
IPD House
Camp Road   0181 946 9100
London SW19 4UX   http: //www.ipd.co.uk

Institute of Practitioners in Advertising
44 Belgrave Square   0171 235 7020
London SW1X 8QS   http: //www.ipa.co.uk

Institute of Professional Investigators
31A Wellington Street
St Johns   01254 680072
Blackburn BB1 8AF   http: //www.ipi.org.uk

Institute of Public Relations, The
The Old Trading House
15 Northburgh Street   0171 253 5151
London EC1V 0PR   http://www.ipr.press.net

Institute of Sales and Marketing Management
Romeland House
Romeland Hill
St Albans
Herts AL3 4ET   01727 812500

Institute of Sales Promotion
Arena House
66–68 Pentonville Road   0171 837 5340
London N1 9HS   http://www.isp.org.uk

Institution of Analysts and Programmers, The
36 Culmington Road   0181 567 2118
London W13 9NH   http://www.iap.org.uk

Institution of Chemical Engineers, The
165 Railway Terrace
Rugby
Warks CV21 3HQ   01788 578214

Institution of Civil Engineers, The
1–7 Great George Street   0171 222 7722
London SW1P 3AA   http://www.ice.org.uk

Institution of Electrical Engineers, The
Savoy Place   0171 240 187
London WC2R 0BL1   http://www.iee.org.uk

Institution of Mechanical Engineers, The
1 Birdcage Walk
London SW1H 9JJ   0171 222 7899

Institution of Structural Engineers, The
11 Upper Belgrave Street
London SW1X 8BH   0171 235 4535

International Consulting Economists Association
3 St George's Court
Putney Bridge Road
London SW15 2PA   0181 875 9960

International Visual Communications Association
Bolsover House
5–6 Clipstone Street   0171 580 0962
London W1P 7EB   http: //www.ivca.com

Managing and Marketing Sales Association
PO Box 11
Sandbach
Cheshire CH11 0DG   01270 526339

Management Consultancies Association
11 West Halkin Street   0171 235 3897
London SW1X 8JL   http: //www.mca.org.uk

Marketing Council, The
Moor Hall
Cookham, Maidenhead   01628 427020
Berks SL6 9QH   http: //www.marketingcouncil.org

Property Consultants Society
107A Tarrant Street
Arundel
West Sussex BN18 7DP   01903 883787

Public Relations Consultants Association
Willow House
Willow Place   0171 233 6026
London SW1P 1JH   http: //www.martex.co.uk/prca

Society of Authors, The
84 Drayton Gardens   0171 373 6642
London SW10 9SB   http: //www.writers.org.uk/society

Society of Competitive Intelligence Professionals
Gordon Donkin
EMG
PO Box 586   01491 419304
High Wycombe HP14 3WJ   http: //www.scip.org

Society of Designer-Craftsmen
24 Rivington Street
London EC2A 3DU   0171 739 3663

Society of Freelance Editors and Proofreaders
Mermaid House
1 Mermaid Court   0171 403 5141
London SE1 1HR   http: //www.sfep.demon.co.uk

Society of Pension Consultants
St Bartholomew House
92 Fleet Street
London EC4Y 1DH   0171 353 1688

Society of Theatre Consultants
47 Bermondsey Street
London SE1 3XF   0171 403 3778

Strategic Planning Society, The
17 Portland Place   0171 636 7737
London W1N 3AF   http: //www.sps.org.uk

Union of Independent Companies
17 Gillingham Street
London SW1V 1HN   0171 630 9796

UK Association of Professional Engineers
Hayes Court
West Common Road
Bromley
Kent BR2 7AU   0181 462 7755

Writers Guild of Great Britain, The
430 Edgware Road   0171 723 8074
London W2 1EH   http: //www.writers.org.uk/guild

Further Reading from Kogan Page

How to Promote Yourself
101 Ways to Better Business Writing, Timothy RV Foster
101 Ways to Get Great Publicity, Timothy RV Foster
101 Ways to Get More Business, Timothy RV Foster
101 Ways to Make More Profits, Steve Pipe
Choosing and Using Management Consultants, Roger Bennet
Effective Presentation Skills, Steve Mandel
How to Communicate Effectively, Bert Decker
How to Develop Assertiveness, Sam R Lloyd
How to Speak and Write Persuasively, Robert Vicar
Sell Your Knowledge: The Professional's Guide to Winning More Business, Monica Nicou, Christine Ribbing and Eva Ading

How to Build Credibility
101 Ways to Better Business Writing, Timothy RV Foster
The Business Guide to Effective Speaking, J Dunckel and E Parnham
The Business Guide to Effective Writing, J Fletcher and DF Gowing
How to Get More Done, John and Fiona Humphrey
Make Every Minute Count, Marion E Haynes

How to Grow the Relationship
101 Ways to Boost Customer Satisfaction, Timothy RV Foster
Customer Service, Malcolm Peel

How to Work with your Clients in the Developmental Stage
101Ways in Better Business Writing, Timothy RV Foster
101 Ways to Generate Great Ideas, Timothy RV Foster
The Art of Creative Thinking, John Adair

Effective Meeting Skills, Marion E Haynes
How to Make Meetings Work, Malcolm Peel
Managing Your Time, Lothar J Seiwert
The Organised Executive, Stephanie Winston
Organizing for the Creative Person, Dorothy Lehmkuhl and
   Dolores Cotter Lamping

How to Work with your Clients in the Ongoing Stage
Report Writing in Business, Trevor J Bentley

How to Work with your Clients when you Have Problems
101 Ways to Better Business Writing, Timothy RV Foster
How to Solve Your People Problems, Jane Allan

Putting It All Together
Going Freelance: Self-Employment With Minimum Capital,
   Godfrey Golzen
How to Set Up and Run Your Own Business, Daily Telegraph
Start and Run a Profitable Consulting Business, Douglas A Gray
Working For Yourself, Godfrey Golzen

Index

INDEX